MY AMAZING DAY

This book belongs to

....

....

....

Every day is amazing.
Every day is an adventure.

Dear Parent,

Every day is amazing. Every day is an adventure. But when your child is at school it can be difficult to know how they are doing. Many parents tell me that when they ask their child how their school day was, they get rather vague answers.

By making a daily journal together my hope is that you will find a better flow of communication.

With best wishes

Libby

Libby J Chatwell

How to use this book

Find a quiet place where you and your child can spend 5 minutes without being interrupted. (that means no TV, computer, iPad, laptop or phone!)

Write in the day and the date (or cut out days (page 100) and stick them in).

Suggest that your child puts a tick or colours the face that shows how they feel. Avoid asking questions e.g. don't say "how do you feel today?", try: "I wonder which face you are going to colour in."

Next, have a look at *Something easy, Something hard, Did anything make me sad?* (see page 99 for prompts to help with thinking). If your child can't think of anything, go straight to drawing something.

When Drawing a picture, avoid asking questions. Try making comments e.g. "That looks like the playground" or "Someone is playing a game".

Lastly, think about things that you are thankful for. (see page 98 for prompts to help with thinking)

- Be like an owl: Observe, wait, listen.
- Make it enjoyable.
- Don't force it - leaving stuff blank is OK.
- Don't insist on your child doing all the writing
- Don't feel guilty if you miss a day just carry on when you can

What was great today?

Today is _____ | Date: _____

How I feel
😊
😐
☹️

Something I loved today / What made me happy?

Something easy

Something hard

Did anything make me sad?

Draw a picture

Things I'm thankful for ...

What was great today?

Today is _____   **Date:** _____

How I feel
- 🙂
- 😐
- 🙁

Something I loved today / What made me happy?

Something easy

Something hard

Did anything make me sad?

Draw a picture

Things I'm thankful for ...

What was great today?

Today is	Date:

How I feel

Something I loved today / What made me happy?

Something easy

Something hard

Did anything make me sad?

Draw a picture

Things I'm thankful for ...

What was great today?

| Today is | Date: |

How I feel

Something I loved today / What made me happy?

Something easy

Something hard

Did anything make me sad?

Draw a picture

Things I'm thankful for ...

What was great today?

| Today is | Date: |

How I feel
- 😊
- 😐
- 😢

Something I loved today / What made me happy?

Something easy

Something hard

Did anything make me sad?

Draw a picture

Things I'm thankful for ...

What was great today?

Today is _____ **Date:** _____

How I feel
- 🙂
- 😐
- ☹️

Something I loved today / What made me happy?

Something easy

Something hard

Did anything make me sad?

Draw a picture

Things I'm thankful for ...

Colour him in

What was great today?

Today is	Date:

How I feel

Something I loved today / What made me happy?

Something easy

Something hard

Did anything make me sad?

Draw a picture

Things I'm thankful for ...

What was great today?

Today is _____ **Date:** _____

How I feel
- 🙂
- 😐
- ☹️

Something I loved today / What made me happy?

Something easy

Something hard

Did anything make me sad?

Draw a picture

Things I'm thankful for ...

What was great today?

Today is _____ **Date:** _____

How I feel
- 🙂
- 😐
- ☹️

Something I loved today / What made me happy?

Something easy

Something hard

Did anything make me sad?

Draw a picture

Things I'm thankful for ...

What was great today?

Today is _____   Date: _____

How I feel

Something I loved today / What made me happy?

Something easy

Something hard

Did anything make me sad?

Draw a picture

Things I'm thankful for ...

What was great today?

Today is	Date:

How I feel

Something I loved today / What made me happy?

Something easy

Something hard

Did anything make me sad?

Draw a picture

Things I'm thankful for ...

Colour him in

What was great today?

Today is _____ **Date:** _____

How I feel
- 😊
- 😐
- ☹️

Something I loved today / What made me happy?

Something easy

Something hard

Did anything make me sad?

Draw a picture

Things I'm thankful for ...

What was great today?

Today is _____   **Date:** _____

How I feel
- 🙂
- 😐
- ☹️

Something I loved today / What made me happy?

Something easy

Something hard

Did anything make me sad?

Draw a picture

Things I'm thankful for ...

What was great today?

Today is _____ **Date:** _____

How I feel
- 🙂
- 😐
- 🙁

Something I loved today / What made me happy?

Something easy

Something hard

Did anything make me sad?

Draw a picture

Things I'm thankful for …

What was great today?

Today is _____ **Date:** _____

How I feel
- 🙂
- 😐
- ☹️

Something I loved today / What made me happy?

Something easy

Something hard

Did anything make me sad?

Draw a picture

Things I'm thankful for ...

What was great today?

Today is	Date:

How I feel

Something I loved today / What made me happy?

Something easy

Something hard

Did anything make me sad?

Draw a picture

Things I'm thankful for ...

Colour him in

What was great today?

| Today is | Date: |

How I feel

Something I loved today / What made me happy?

Something easy

Something hard

Did anything make me sad?

Draw a picture

Things I'm thankful for ...

What was great today?

Today is _____   Date: _____

How I feel

Something I loved today / What made me happy?

Something easy

Something hard

Did anything make me sad?

Draw a picture

Things I'm thankful for ...

What was great today?

Today is

Date:

How I feel

Something I loved today / What made me happy?

Something easy

Something hard

Did anything make me sad?

Draw a picture

Things I'm thankful for ...

What was great today?

Today is **Date:**

How I feel

Something I loved today / What made me happy?

Something easy

Something hard

Did anything make me sad?

Draw a picture

Things I'm thankful for ...

What was great today?

| Today is | Date: |

How I feel

Something I loved today / What made me happy?

Something easy

Something hard

Did anything make me sad?

Draw a picture

Things I'm thankful for ...

How many dinosaurs?

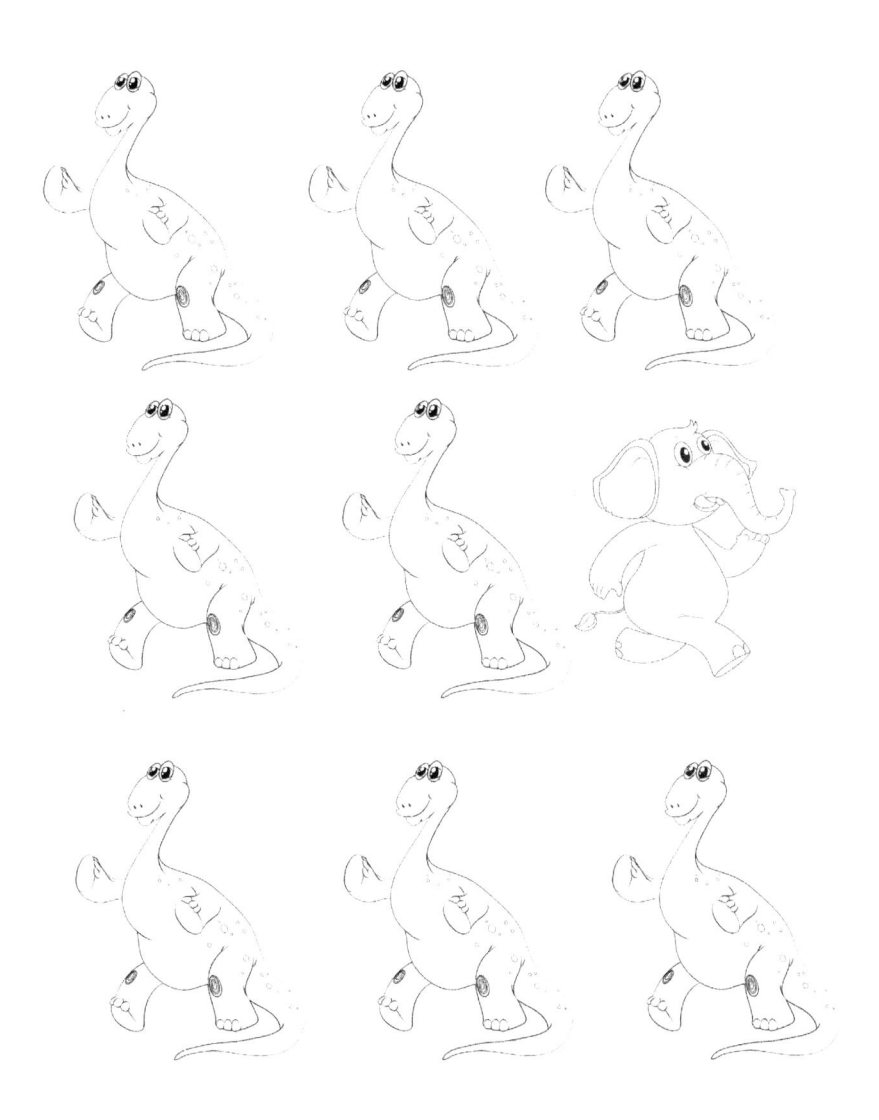

What was great today?

| Today is | Date: |

How I feel
- 🙂
- 😐
- ☹️

Something I loved today / What made me happy?

Something easy

Something hard

Did anything make me sad?

Draw a picture

Things I'm thankful for ...

What was great today?

Today is _____ **Date:** _____

How I feel
- 🙂
- 😐
- ☹️

Something I loved today / What made me happy?

Something easy

Something hard

Did anything make me sad?

Draw a picture

Things I'm thankful for ...

What was great today?

| Today is | Date: |

How I feel

Something I loved today / What made me happy?

Something easy

Something hard

Did anything make me sad?

Draw a picture

Things I'm thankful for ...

What was great today?

Today is _____ **Date:** _____

How I feel
- 😊
- 😐
- 😢

Something I loved today / What made me happy?

Something easy

Something hard

Did anything make me sad?

Draw a picture

Things I'm thankful for ...

What was great today?

Today is

Date:

How I feel

Something I loved today / What made me happy?

Something easy

Something hard

Did anything make me sad?

Draw a picture

Things I'm thankful for ...

A picture of me

Draw a picture
- make sure you look in the mirror!
Now, do a picture of a brother, a sister, a friend. What's different?
What's the same?

What was great today?

| Today is | Date: |

How I feel

Something I loved today / What made me happy?

Something easy

Something hard

Did anything make me sad?

Draw a picture

Things I'm thankful for ...

What was great today?

Today is _____ **Date:** _____

How I feel
- 🙂
- 😐
- ☹️

Something I loved today / What made me happy?

Something easy

Something hard

Did anything make me sad?

Draw a picture

Things I'm thankful for ...

What was great today?

Today is _____ **Date:** _____

How I feel

Something I loved today / What made me happy?

Something easy

Something hard

Did anything make me sad?

Draw a picture

Things I'm thankful for ...

What was great today?

Today is **Date:**

How I feel

Something I loved today / What made me happy?

Something easy

Something hard

Did anything make me sad?

Draw a picture

Things I'm thankful for ...

What was great today?

Today is _____   **Date:** _____

How I feel
- 🙂
- 😐
- 🙁

Something I loved today / What made me happy?

Something easy

Something hard

Did anything make me sad?

Draw a picture

Things I'm thankful for ...

What was great today?

Today is _____ **Date:** _____

How I feel
🙂
😐
☹️

Something I loved today / What made me happy?

Something easy

Something hard

Did anything make me sad?

Draw a picture

Things I'm thankful for …

Food I like

Make a list of food you like or grab a free magazine from the supermarket and cut out pictures and stick them here.

Is there something you haven't tried or aren't sure of? Why not give something new a go?

Note to parent:
Make a small portion of a new food available for your child to try, without any pressure. It may take a few tries before they get to like it.

What was great today?

Today is _____   **Date:** _____

How I feel
- 😊
- 😐
- ☹️

Something I loved today / What made me happy?

Something easy

Something hard

Did anything make me sad?

Draw a picture

Things I'm thankful for ...

What was great today?

Today is _____ **Date:** _____

How I feel
- 🙂
- 😐
- ☹️

Something I loved today / What made me happy?

Something easy

Something hard

Did anything make me sad?

Draw a picture

Things I'm thankful for ...

What was great today?

| Today is | Date: |

How I feel
- 🙂
- 😐
- 🙁

Something I loved today / What made me happy?

Something easy

Something hard

Did anything make me sad?

Draw a picture

Things I'm thankful for ...

What was great today?

Today is _____ **Date:** _____

How I feel

Something I loved today / What made me happy?

Something easy

Something hard

Did anything make me sad?

Draw a picture

Things I'm thankful for ...

What was great today?

| Today is | Date: |

How I feel

Something I loved today / What made me happy?

Something easy

Something hard

Did anything make me sad?

Draw a picture

Things I'm thankful for ...

Be kind

Think of something you could do to be kind: Maybe you could take turns with a brother, sister or friend or let them choose which TV to watch.

Note to parent:
Try to catch your child doing something kind or helpful. When you do, say e.g. "You tidied up your toys, that was very helpful".
Noticing and commenting on good behaviour when it happens is very powerful.

What was great today?

Today is _____ **Date:** _____

How I feel
- 🙂
- 😐
- ☹️

Something I loved today / What made me happy?

Something easy

Something hard

Did anything make me sad?

Draw a picture

Things I'm thankful for ...

What was great today?

Today is _____ **Date:** _____

How I feel
- 🙂
- 😐
- ☹️

Something I loved today / What made me happy?

Something easy

Something hard

Did anything make me sad?

Draw a picture

Things I'm thankful for ...

What was great today?

Today is

Date:

How I feel

Something I loved today / What made me happy?

Something easy

Something hard

Did anything make me sad?

Draw a picture

Things I'm thankful for ...

What was great today?

Today is	Date:

How I feel
- 🙂
- 😐
- 🙁

Something I loved today / What made me happy?

Something easy

Something hard

Did anything make me sad?

Draw a picture

Things I'm thankful for ...

What was great today?

Today is _____ **Date:** _____

How I feel
- 🙂
- 😐
- ☹️

Something I loved today / What made me happy?

Something easy

Something hard

Did anything make me sad?

Draw a picture

Things I'm thankful for ...

Stuff I'm good at

Make a list of the things you can do by yourself. Maybe there's something you want to get better at doing?

Note to parent:
Learning independence skills boosts a child's self esteem. Take some time to teach and praise new skills .e.g making a sandwich, spreading honey on toast, putting her/his plate in the dishwasher.

What was great today?

Today is | **Date:**

How I feel

Something I loved today / What made me happy?

Something easy

Something hard

Did anything make me sad?

Draw a picture

Things I'm thankful for ...

What was great today?

| Today is | Date: |

How I feel

Something I loved today / What made me happy?

Something easy

Something hard

Did anything make me sad?

Draw a picture

Things I'm thankful for ...

What was great today?

Today is _____ **Date:** _____

How I feel
- 🙂
- 😐
- ☹️

Something I loved today / What made me happy?

Something easy

Something hard

Did anything make me sad?

Draw a picture

Things I'm thankful for ...

What was great today?

Today is

Date:

How I feel

Something I loved today / What made me happy?

Something easy

Something hard

Did anything make me sad?

Draw a picture

Things I'm thankful for ...

What was great today?

Today is _____   Date: _____

How I feel
😊
😐
☹

Something I loved today / What made me happy?

Something easy

Something hard

Did anything make me sad?

Draw a picture

Things I'm thankful for ...

Things I like doing

Make a list of the things you like doing. Here are some ideas.

IPAD GAMES
YOUTUBE
COLOURING
DANCING
RUNNING
DANCING
PARTIES
SINGING
SOCCER
FOOTBALL
DINOSAUR GAMES
PLAYING
WATCHING TV

What was great today?

Today is _____ **Date:** _____

How I feel
- 🙂
- 😐
- ☹️

Something I loved today / What made me happy?

Something easy

Something hard

Did anything make me sad?

Draw a picture

Things I'm thankful for ...

What was great today?

Today is _____ **Date:** _____

How I feel
- 🙂
- 😐
- ☹️

Something I loved today / What made me happy?

Something easy

Something hard

Did anything make me sad?

Draw a picture

Things I'm thankful for ...

What was great today?

| Today is | Date: |

How I feel

Something I loved today / What made me happy?

Something easy

Something hard

Did anything make me sad?

Draw a picture

Things I'm thankful for ...

What was great today?

Today is _____ **Date:** _____

How I feel
- 😊
- 😐
- ☹️

Something I loved today / What made me happy?

Something easy

Something hard

Did anything make me sad?

Draw a picture

Things I'm thankful for ...

What was great today?

Today is | **Date:**

How I feel

Something I loved today / What made me happy?

Something easy

Something hard

Did anything make me sad?

Draw a picture

Things I'm thankful for ...

Make a story

Make a story about your weekend. Here are some ideas.

WHERE?
- IN THE PARK
- AT THE SHOPS
- IN THE KITCHEN

WHO?
- MUM
- A WIZARD
- ME

WHAT HAPPENED?
- SAW A SPIDER
- RODE A BIKE
- ATE AN ICE CREAM

What was great today?

Today is _____ **Date:** _____

How I feel

Something I loved today / What made me happy?

Something easy

Something hard

Did anything make me sad?

Draw a picture

Things I'm thankful for ...

What was great today?

Today is _____ **Date:** _____

How I feel

Something I loved today / What made me happy?

Something easy

Something hard

Did anything make me sad?

Draw a picture

Things I'm thankful for ...

What was great today?

| Today is | Date: |

How I feel

Something I loved today / What made me happy?

Something easy

Something hard

Did anything make me sad?

Draw a picture

Things I'm thankful for ...

What was great today?

Today is _____ **Date:** _____

How I feel
- 😊
- 😐
- ☹️

Something I loved today / What made me happy?

Something easy

Something hard

Did anything make me sad?

Draw a picture

Things I'm thankful for ...

What was great today?

Today is _____ Date: _____

How I feel
- 🙂
- 😐
- ☹️

Something I loved today / What made me happy?

Something easy

Something hard

Did anything make me sad?

Draw a picture

Things I'm thankful for ...

Play categories

Cutout the cards and place them face down in a pile. Take turns to turn over a card and role a die. The number on the die tells you how many things you have to name in the category.

Farm animals	Sports
Things with wheels	Musical instruments
Types of clothing	Types of fruit
Jungle animals	Things in the kitchen
Types of vegetable	Things that fly

What was great today?

Today is _____ **Date:** _____

How I feel
- 🙂
- 😐
- ☹️

Something I loved today / What made me happy?

Something easy

Something hard

Did anything make me sad?

Draw a picture

Things I'm thankful for ...

What was great today?

| Today is | Date: |

How I feel

Something I loved today / What made me happy?

Something easy

Something hard

Did anything make me sad?

Draw a picture

Things I'm thankful for ...

What was great today?

| Today is | Date: |

How I feel

Something I loved today / What made me happy?

Something easy

Something hard

Did anything make me sad?

Draw a picture

Things I'm thankful for ...

What was great today?

Today is _____   **Date:** _____

How I feel

Something I loved today / What made me happy?

Something easy

Something hard

Did anything make me sad?

Draw a picture

Things I'm thankful for ...

What was great today?

Today is _____ **Date:** _____

How I feel
- 🙂
- 😐
- 🙁

Something I loved today / What made me happy?

Something easy

Something hard

Did anything make me sad?

Draw a picture

Things I'm thankful for ...

A picture of my family

Draw a picture of your family. Draw the people that live with you first. Then think about others e.g. cousins, uncles, aunts, grandma, grandad and add them in.

What is each person's favourite dinner? If you don't know, go and ask them.

What was great today?

| Today is | Date: |

How I feel

Something I loved today / What made me happy?

Something easy

Something hard

Did anything make me sad?

Draw a picture

Things I'm thankful for ...

What was great today?

Today is

Date:

How I feel

Something I loved today / What made me happy?

Something easy

Something hard

Did anything make me sad?

Draw a picture

Things I'm thankful for ...

What was great today?

Today is

Date:

How I feel

Something I loved today / What made me happy?

Something easy

Something hard

Did anything make me sad?

Draw a picture

Things I'm thankful for ...

What was great today?

Today is _____   **Date:** _____

How I feel
🙂
😐
☹️

Something I loved today / What made me happy?

Something easy

Something hard

Did anything make me sad?

Draw a picture

Things I'm thankful for ...

What was great today?

Today is _____ **Date:** _____

How I feel

Something I loved today / What made me happy?

Something easy

Something hard

Did anything make me sad?

Draw a picture

Things I'm thankful for ...

Where I live

Draw a picture of your house. What else is near your house: a shop, a park, a bus stop, a train station, your school. See if you can draw a little map with all the places in your neighbourhood.

What was great today?

Today is _____ Date: _____

How I feel
😊
😐
☹️

Something I loved today / What made me happy?

Something easy

Something hard

Did anything make me sad?

Draw a picture

Things I'm thankful for ...

What was great today?

Today is _____ **Date:** _____

How I feel

Something I loved today / What made me happy?

Something easy

Something hard

Did anything make me sad?

Draw a picture

Things I'm thankful for ...

What was great today?

| Today is | Date: |

How I feel

Something I loved today / What made me happy?

Something easy

Something hard

Did anything make me sad?

Draw a picture

Things I'm thankful for ...

What was great today?

| Today is | Date: |

How I feel

Something I loved today / What made me happy?

Something easy

Something hard

Did anything make me sad?

Draw a picture

Things I'm thankful for ...

What was great today?

Today is

Date:

How I feel

Something I loved today / What made me happy?

Something easy

Something hard

Did anything make me sad?

Draw a picture

Things I'm thankful for ...

Colour him in

What was great today?

Today is   Date:

How I feel

Something I loved today / What made me happy?

Something easy

Something hard

Did anything make me sad?

Draw a picture

Things I'm thankful for ...

What was great today?

Today is _____ **Date:** _____

How I feel
- 🙂
- 😐
- ☹️

Something I loved today / What made me happy?

Something easy

Something hard

Did anything make me sad?

Draw a picture

Things I'm thankful for …

What was great today?

Today is _____ **Date:** _____

How I feel
- 🙂
- 😐
- ☹️

Something I loved today / What made me happy?

Something easy

Something hard

Did anything make me sad?

Draw a picture

Things I'm thankful for ...

What was great today?

Today is

Date:

How I feel

Something I loved today / What made me happy?

Something easy

Something hard

Did anything make me sad?

Draw a picture

Things I'm thankful for ...

What was great today?

Today is _____ **Date:** _____

How I feel
- 🙂
- 😐
- ☹️

Something I loved today / What made me happy?

Something easy

Something hard

Did anything make me sad?

Draw a picture

Things I'm thankful for ...

What was great today?

Today is _____   **Date:** _____

How I feel
- 🙂
- 😐
- 🙁

Something I loved today / What made me happy?

Something easy

Something hard

Did anything make me sad?

Draw a picture

Things I'm thankful for ...

What was great today?

Today is	Date:

How I feel

Something I loved today / What made me happy?

Something easy

Something hard

Did anything make me sad?

Draw a picture

Things I'm thankful for ...

Ideas for "Things I'm thankful for"

PAINTING
LEGO
TOY CARS
FAMILY
IPAD
CAKES
CEREAL
WATERMELON
DANCING
CUTE ANIMALS
CARS
FRIENDS
SINGING
TOYS
CHOCOLATE
BANANAS
NURSES
TEACHERS
MILK
TRAINS
COOKIES
MOVIES

Ideas for Easy and Hard things

LISTENING   READING   REGISTER
RE   PHONICS   TELLING NEWS
DRAWING
CIRCLE TIME   LUNCHTIME
PLAYTIME
LINING UP   WAITING FOR MY TURN
NUMBERS
WRITING
SINGING
LOOKING   MATHS   TALKING TO FRIENDS
TEACHERS
ASSEMBLY   PE
ANSWERING QUESTIONS   MUSIC
ASKING FOR HELP

Days of the week

Sunday	Sunday	Sunday
Monday	Monday	Monday
Tuesday	Tuesday	Tuesday
Wednesday	Wednesday	Wednesday
Thursday	Thursday	Thursday
Friday	Friday	Friday
Saturday	Saturday	Saturday
Sunday	Sunday	Sunday
Monday	Monday	Monday
Tuesday	Tuesday	Tuesday
Wednesday	Wednesday	Wednesday
Thursday	Thursday	Thursday
Friday	Friday	Friday
Saturday	Saturday	Saturday

Printed in Great Britain
by Amazon